D0891502

THE GOOD
IN
EXISTENTIAL
METAPHYSICS

Aquinas Lecture, 1952

THE GOOD
IN
EXISTENTIAL
METAPHYSICS

Under the Auspices of the Aristotelian Society
of Marquette University

BY

ELIZABETH G. SALMON, Doct. en phil.

MARQUETTE UNIVERSITY PRESS
MILWAUKEE
1953

B
765
.T5A6
1952

To My Mother — March 16th

PREFATORY

The Aristotelian Society of Marquette University each year invites a scholar to deliver a lecture in honor of St. Thomas Aquinas. Customarily delivered on the Sunday nearest March 7, the feast day of the Society's patron saint, these lectures are called the Aquinas lectures.

In 1952 the Society had the honor of recording the lecture of Elizabeth G. Salmon, associate professor of philosophy in the Graduate School of Fordham University.

Miss Salmon was born in New York City. Having entered the College of Mount St. Vincent-on-the-Hudson with a New York Regents State Scholarship she was graduated with an A.B. summa cum laude. For a year and a half she took courses at the Sorbonne of the University of Paris, the École des Hautes Études and the Institut Catholique de Paris, attending the classes of Etienne Gilson and Jacques Maritain. She then attended the Institut Supérieur de Philosophie at the University of Louvain, in Belgium, receiving the degree of Docteur en Philosophie with honors.

She was assistant professor of philosophy at the College of Mount St. Vincent for a year. She lectured in philosophy at the College of the Sacred Heart Manhattanville the following year. Then she became lecturer in the Graduate School of Fordham University. The following year she became assistant professor and is now associate professor of philosophy in the Fordham Graduate School.

Miss Salmon was vice-president of the American Catholic Philosophical Association in 1951-52 and president 1952-53. She is also a member of the Metaphysical Society of America and a fellow of the C.R.B. Educational Foundation.

She has contributed to scholarly journals including *Thought* and *The New Scholasticism*. Articles by her have appeared in the *Proceedings of the American Catholic Philosophical Association* and the *Proceedings of the American Catholic Educational Association*.

THE GOOD
IN
EXISTENTIAL
METAPHYSICS

The Good in
Existential Metaphysics

THE Good—it seems to convey such a simple notion. Most of us take it for granted. Yet we can still remember when we thought candy was very good but Mother said it wasn't good for us and we were punished when we ate it behind her back. And all that complexity had to do with candy that was very sweet and, we thought, very good. Broadly speaking, there are two general notions involved: the metaphysical or ontological notion of the good, the thing as sweet, which is basic, and the moral notion, the forbidden sweet, the good but not for us.

Maritain says of the ontological good in *Les Sept Lecons sur l'Etre*: "The notion of the good is a primary notion, as any transcendental notion which suddenly arises under a certain angle of vision, in order to reveal a new face of being, a new intelligible mystery consubstantial with being."[1]

This description of the good raises a few reflections. What is the meaning of primary when one is considering a metaphysical notion? Is the metaphysical significance given immediately to the mind? What is the meaning of primary in relation to transcendental notions when these notions have a certain order? What, may we ask, is the angle of vision under which the notion of the good arises? It is not apparently given in the vision of being. In fact, what is an angle of vision? Moreover if the notion of the good arises from a vision how is it said that it is a new and not the primary face of being? How is it a primary and yet a new intelligible mystery? Also it is consubstantial with being and yet is gained by a certain angle of vision. Reflecting on this description it is evident that the notion of the good as a transcendental notion has a certain complexity. Moreover the notion of the good does not end with the transcendental notion as we saw in our little example. Rather it is almost inevitable that the notion of moral goodness would come to mind even before that of the transcendental notion of the good. But how are these two notions called good? Is not moral goodness something that is also primary? How then are the notions incorporated one in the other? It is our task to try to plumb the meanings of the good in metaphysics and the fundamental notion of moral goodness as connected with the metaphysical good.

It would be impossible to give the whole basis of a transcendental notion. Only a few fundamental ideas that will lead us to the transcendental notion of the good will be touched upon.

First of all, no fundamental metaphysical notion is given or seen with its specifically metaphysical significance on our first apprehension of being. In that sense no metaphysical notion is primary. However it is primary in the sense that it is seen immediately, not developed through an argument and so not held as a conclusion. Being, it is true, is given in all and every knowledge experience but its strictly metaphysical significance is not evident to us except through much reflection on that experience. It is seen in an explicit intelligibility of intellectual knowledge, that is, an explicit intelligibility of the judgment. This sight is gained by reflecting for further understanding upon the intelligibility rendered intelligible in our judgments. As Father Robert Henle has expressed it, "Metaphysics must . . . be derived from experience, through a constantly purifying reflection . . . the fundamental necessities and intelligibilities with which metaphysics deals, and on which it builds must be continually discovered in concrete experience."[2] But, we may add, it is concrete experience rendered intelligible through mind actually knowing and desiring.

This insight, resulting from a constantly purifying reflection, is a vision but since it is a vision of being as rendered intelligible and this, for us, is only through abstractive knowledge it could be called an abstractive vision. But as the abstractive vision is a vision of actual existing being, as intellectually expressed in the existential judgment, it is seen as a primary understanding. As we slowly reflect on the **intelligibility of our existential judgments**[3] **we realize that** a being to be being has a certain significance, and we come to a notion of being as being, a notion that transcends all classes or kinds, and expresses an intelligibility of anything that is or could be a being. As we shall see it is a notion that grasps a certain understanding of all that is. It so gives a unified understanding which is an understanding also of a certain unity in being, but yet it is an understanding that must respect the diver-

sity of what is and so possesses the very
minimum of unity. We express this by saying this notion is analogical. The constantly purifying reflection is the developing of
a *habitus* of balancing this unity and diversity in one notion which is not strictly a
notion as in the univocal concept.

Moreover it is very important to note
that the order in the transcendental notions
mark a development in our reflections.‖ To
say that the transcendental notions are distinct from each other by a distinction of
reason is, besides other things, to stress the
discursive, non-intuitive, development of
the understanding of our intellectual in-
sights‖ Looked at from another angle it
underlines the richness of being in which
all these aspects or intelligible insights are
fused in unity.[4] This unity in its richness
is seized by us only by constant reflection,
by the gradual development of new abstractive visions which, as abstractive and
non-intuitive visions, reveal through their

intelligibility a further depth of mystery, the mystery of being.

Now the transcendental notion of the good is one that St. Thomas puts as coming after the notion of being, the one, and the true.[5] He puts the good in this order because he sees the notion as presupposing the reflections and resulting from the abstractive visions that are seen in these previous notions. Thus the notion of the good is, to a discursive mind, less primary and more complex than the previous notions. Yet it can be called a primary notion in as much as it is a development of the first transcendental notion, a deepening of it, without being a conclusion from more primary principles. Thus for us the notion of the transcendental good arises suddenly, immediately in a primary manner under a certain angle of vision, that is, an angle that develops upon our understanding of being, unity and truth. We must pull, as it were, the intelligibility of being, unity and truth into our abstractive intuition of the notion of the good.[6]

The problem is: what exactly is the intelligibility that we amass in the notion of the good? Trying to show what it is will also make evident that the order of the transcendentals is an essential factor in this understanding.

First of all *being* stresses the absolute position of what is; it stresses it as an existent, and in the existent the act of existence is the "actuality of all things even of forms themselves."[7] An existent or being is an existing or actual *form* or *essence*. When this is recognized as the very condition or law of everything that is, there is formed the transcendental notion of being. It can also be stressed that anything that is, having the ultimate act of existence has a certain necessity, a self-sufficiency, and that the act of "to be" is the root of these characteristics. Also all things are alike, with an analogical likeness through this act of "to be." All beings are, but yet all are ac-

cording to their manner of being. All
beings are something by or in reference to,
the act of existence but all are also seen as
this or that mode of existence. Thus the
vague unity of existence is only through
the richness of diversity. Thus with the
notion of *ens* we are faced with actual subsistent existent with its degree of necessity.
    But from this reflection on being, we
slip as it were to another angle of vision
and note that what is, in and through its
act of "to be," is one.[8] Because it is, it is
itself, and not other. The actual subsistent
is one. Often the notion of the unity of
being is stressed solely from the point of
view of essence. It is true that from that
point of view a being is one. The essence
of being is often spoken of as non-contradictory, but do not the essential notes hang
together as non-contradictory because it
is that mode of being? In other words, because a thing *is* that being, its essence is
that essence and so can be seen from the
point of view of truth as a non-contradic-

tory unity. But that is an angle of unity explicit only after the development of the
notion of truth.

Unity as a transcendental notion shows
us that whatever is, in as much as it is, is
one and distinct from each and every other
being. But also, since it is seen that all
beings are in a vague way alike as beings,
so too all beings are vaguely one as being.
There is no outside to the universe of being
except blank nothing. This vague notion
of unity hints at the idea that the many of
being must be unified and related under
the pain of contradicting the meaning of
being. There is a certain lack of completeness in the many.

As these reflections are absorbed, a
new vision comes almost immediately to
the fore, like a new flash in a swiftly moving cinema. A being is; to be is to be
something; to be something is to be a unit;
that is, itself and not other. We reflect that
whatever is, is; it is what it is; it cannot be
and not be at the same time. We are de-

limiting being within being. Moreover these notions express the very law or character of being. And immediately we see, as in a vision, that we are understanding this; we are understanding being. But what is more important than our immediate reflection is that we see being as understandable in being understood.[9] Being, in as much as it is being, is intelligible; it is not rendered intelligible by something else; being is intelligible clarity;[10] but one may have trouble seizing that very clarity.[11] Being is seen as the foundation of any actual truth of mind. And this must be the characterization of the whole field of being as being. So being as being must be that which is always included in the field of the intelligible, as the source and basis of a relation to an intellect; it is connatural to intellect. Being itself is true.

Yet in considering discussions on ontological truth we often meet the problem of the transcendental notion of the true explained in immediate relation of the Divine

Mind and this before the proof of the existence of God. However there is a certain
understanding of being as being or *ens* and
its intelligibility before developing the
the proof of the existence of God; just as
we see being as act is one and vaguely all
being as being is one before the plurality
of created being is reduced to its full intelligible unity in the first cause.[12]

As Maritain stresses it, the true is being
answering to, speaking to, expressing itself,
manifesting itself to the knowing mind.[13]
It is act as intelligible. A finite act may be
paradoxical but in as much as it is, it is
intelligible, and being in as much as it is
being is seen as true.

Having reflected this much, we realize
that a beyond-all-that-is, is nothing, no-
being; that the absolute chaos of disunity
in which nothing is itself is a mental night-
mare; that the possibility of the pure negation of being, of that which is contradic-
tory cannot be. The beyond-of-being is a
void of emptiness, disorder, madness that

we can't even conceive because it doesn't exist. Through a continuing reflection, a contemplation of act and primarily of "that act of existence as the perfection of all perfections" a new angle of vision develops. Slowly we have seen that existence constitutes the "isness" of a thing: makes it to be: that it is the primary principle of unity; the primary condition of intelligibility, of the ability to be known. Moreover, considering the void that is the opposite of being, we suddenly realize to a certain degree that "*esse enim actu in unoquoque est bonum ipsius*"[14] or "*esse igitur actu boni rationem constituit.*"[15]

In other words, the growing realization of what is the significance of actuality brings us to the realization that to be actual, to be something that exists, is what makes a thing good. That does not mean that the *ratio* of being is the same as the *ratio* of the good. Rather it means the *ratio* of the good is an understanding of being, unity and truth not only as seen in the unity of a concrete being but as gradually understood of such a being in its various aspects and its connection with all other being. And in this understanding there is always an appetitive non-knowledge factor implicitly included but only as it is referred to explicitly does the notion of the good develop clearly.[16]

As much as the notion of the good seems to flow easily from the true, as the next development of a reflective vision, yet there are some complexities about it that make it difficult to understand fully. The problem is: what exactly is the *"bonum"*?

St. Thomas says: "Now just as the actually colored is the object of sight, so good is the object of the will. Therefore if the will be offered an object which is good universally and from every point of view, the will tends to it of necessity, if it wills anything at all; since it cannot will the opposite."[17]

So it is the good that moves the will. Moreover he says "that which is apprehended under the nature or *ratio* of what is good and befitting moves the will as an object."[18]

What is to be noted is that the object of the will is the good. But also the *apprehended good* is what specifies the will and moves it to tend. We often think we love being and then see it as good, but rather, it seems we apprehend it as good then tend and love and rest in it. But does the actuation of the will, its movement and especially the act of love mean nothing in the development of the transcendental notion of the good? If it does, it seems that the notion of the good is given without any mention of this last act of the will; it seems that the intellect apprehends the good, and the good can be defined without reference to intellective appetite. The difficulty will perhaps be clarified in considering the genesis of the notion of the good leading to the understanding of being as good.

As was mentioned in reference to the transcendental n o t i o n of b e i n g, it is

through reflection on existential judgments
that we come to appreciate existence as the
act of all acts. Our existential judgments
terminate, through reflection on sense
knowledge, in an existing thing. But the
notion of being results from an intellectual
apprehension first of being as essence of
a thing or the *ratio* of the species and then
further this essence is understood as that
of the existing thing, and the actuality of
existence is expressed in the judgment, but
it is existence as understood. So both of
these views of being, as essence or existence, as intelligible, could be considered as
included in the *ratio* of the species. And
St. Thomas says that a thing is perfected
"in one manner according to the *ratio* of
the species only; and thus intellect which
is perfected by the *ratio* of being, is perfected by being."[19] But being is not in its
natural existence present in intellect, so its
actual existence as such does not perfect
intellect. St. Thomas adds in another way
"being is perfective of another, not alone

according to the *ratio* of the species, but even according to the *esse* which it has in the nature of things; and in this manner is the good perfective."[20]

Being then, through its actual existence and this as perfective of being in some manner, is the aspect of being which is designated as good.[21] Though this shows us that apparently the good has an extremely existential connotation yet it also raises difficulties in trying to conceive the notion as having a transcendental significance. And what we are looking for is the full and exact significance of what we mean by the good as good and the good as interchangeable with being.

Now man's most developed knowledge, the metaphysical significance of being and so of the good is obtained, as has been noted, by a continuing reflection on his own knowing and also, we must now stress, on his own desiring. In the experience reflected on, there has been a process of knowing together with the non-knowledge factor of appetite and the ensuing reflection has in it, implicitly, this total experience. In trying to discern the meaning we have in our most developed reflection we must make explicit what we are carrying along in the experience reflected on, and make it, if we can, explicit. Thus apprehensions of intellect can have in them an appreciation of the result of appetite on a lower level, and the meanings connected with lower levels of being are carried over, at least in an analogous fashion, into the more developed meaning. Let us try to trace this development.

As M. Gilson remarks, man is a cause (and so a being) in various ways: in the manner of a physical body; in the manner of a living and organized body, and also in the manner of a reasonable being.[22] Moreover man, as intellectual, is able to reflect upon himself in act, and to a certain degree understand his act, his tendencies and through them to a certain degree understand his nature. [23] So he can study himself as a physical, sensible and intellectual being. Man sees himself as a physico-sensible being open to physical influences but also himself as a physical being having certain inclinations or directions to some other things. Any such inclination he has naturally from his nature as a physical thing. St. Thomas calls it a natural tendency to something that is suitable.[24] This tendency is determined to a particular thing. It is a tendency of one physical existent to be connected with another physical thing or physical situation. Or perhaps more correctly the whole physical world as existent is to be as moved and moving, or to be as a part acting and as a part reacting. Thus the movement to a determined effect or the inclination to it, is in line with a development of physical being, a completion of its actuality through the physical existence of and effect upon, other things. The "to be" of the physical universe is to be not as assimilating other things, but as joining to form a whole. Strictly speaking a physical being doesn't exactly tend to something suitable to it. It is more an interaction of parts to maintain the whole. The being to be maintained and completed is the being of the physical universe rather than one physical existent with respect to another. So the suitable is the suitability of one part to the other part for the maintenance and completion of the whole. The thing as suitable here is not so much perfective of another by its existence as it is perfective as parts are of a whole. Thus at this stage there really is no distinguishing of the suitable from the non-suitable; there is no turning away. What is evident is the active order and connectedness which maintains the being of the universe. If one says the natural inclination flows from the form, it is in this case the form of the species; the individuals are this form in quantified parts and diversified forces—more relational than individual.

Man, besides being a physical being, is a sensitive being. Acted upon by the physical universe he does not react entirely like a physical thing but he reacts as a whole, living organism with certain means to seek or avoid what is helpful or harmful to him. With sense consciousness there is a certain awareness of his unity and instinctive tendency to preserve it. With sense knowledge he becomes aware of what is suitable and non-suitable, not as considering the character of suitableness as such but as perceiving suitable things here and now under certain sensible aspects. Under these aspects he tends toward the thing or flees from it.[25]

It is through sense knowledge which includes perception, imagination and the aestimative sense, that sense appetite is awakened. For as St. Thomas says "the motion of the appetitive part arises in some manner from apprehension because every operation of a passive power has its origin from an active power."[26] Again he says "the appetible in truth does not move appetite unless apprehended."[27] Now the problem is: what is apprehended? In something that is desired two things can be considered: the thing which is desired and the *ratio* of appetibility.

In physical or natural tendencies there is no distinction between the thing and the *ratio* of appetibility, or the aspect of desirability. Where there is knowledge there is a certain distinction. With sense knowledge something is apprehended as pleasing to sense and there is a sense appetite for anything of that category with those pleasing sensible aspects, i.e., a sense appetite will tend toward any singular thing of that kind in the particular sensible condition here and now of the perceiving animal. The animal will turn from any category that is harmful. Thus it is not determined just to one thing independently of its aspect of suitability or nonsuitability, but it is determined to tend to it when it is perceived as suitable. There is, however, no perception of suitability as such apart from the thing. Yet sense is not determined to the thing apart from a perception of suitability. Thus sense perception perceives a concrete thing with a certain aspect such as sweet food. What is perceived is a thing whose sensible aspect makes it known that when tasted it is sweet. What can be desired if the animal needs it, is the sweetness and this is perfective as actually being tasted; it is not perfective just from being perceived. It is not that sense knowledge perceives the sweetness as sweetness and so specifies appetite. Rather it perceives the *ratio* of the desired, or *ratio* of sweetness, not apart from, but in the thing; it perceives an aspect sensibly known, that given to a certain sense appetite will actuate the appetite to tend to it as sweet and so be suited. So, though in sense knowledge there is not any knowledge of the distinction between the thing and the *ratio appetibilis*, we can at least see the important distinction between the thing perceived under its aspect of suitability and the thing as it actuates the appetite.

Here certainly in the sensible order beings in their sensible concrete existence are assimilated by the perceiving animal in view of fulfilling his needs and so completing, perfecting or maintaining his being— and they are marked strongly by the subjective character of sense knowledge. So those things or beings that are suitable to the animal could be called good. Thus being would be divided not as good and non-good as corresponding to being and non-being, but rather as the suitable and the non-suitable. It is a division of being relative to the sense appetite and its particular nature.[28] At this level it would be better perhaps to speak always of the suitable and non-suitable rather than of the good.

Man as intellectual is able to reflect and know his own nature to a degree. He can reflect on himself knowing, sensibly and intellectually and upon the union of the two in his own nature. He also can reflect on the appetitive reaction to this knowledge.

The first mark of intellectual knowledge is its independence; it immediately transcends the situation. Man through his intellect looks upon himself as sensible, and distinguishes the knowledge and appetitive factors in his activity. More than that he distinguishes on the one hand the sensible thing as a thing, that can as a thing or *res* be considered in itself and on the other hand the *ratio* of appetibility or the aspect under which it is desirable. This is possible because he can see the thing as not essentially identical with an aspect that appeals to some sense appetite. He does not understand the thing to be its sweetness. But there is a thing that has that about it which can answer to the desire or need of sweetness. Through sensible aspects that can appeal to certain sense appetites the mind of man seizes being as a nature, as a source from which these aspects flow. It also recognizes that in their physical existence these things with properties which are suitable fill and satisfy his sense appetites.

But the object of intellect itself is *quod quid est* and it extends itself to all those things that have a quiddity. In other words intellect, seeing things as being or quiddity or nature, can distinguish a thing as nature and the sensible aspect that serves as the *ratio* of desirability. It can distinguish a thing as something or *res* from its aspects of suitability or non-suitability. Intellect can unify the suitable and non-suitable as united in things or nature. Both aspects are rooted in quiddities or natures.

Now since man can know things as natures isn't there an appetite that follows upon such knowledge? It is now no longer a question of sense appetite but rational appetite. But mind grasps it under what *ratio* of appetibility?

For a moment let us look at the appetite with which we are dealing. It is a tendency, according to St. Thomas, that is immediately aroused in the soul upon that soul knowing in act.[29] It is an appetite that follows upon reason. In fact we call it rational appetite and this is not parallel with reason but rather it shoots off from it. If it is a rational appetite it is going to desire the rational, the intelligible. As appetite we can see from the lower levels it is going to desire or tend to act, to being as existing as perfective of it.

Now to tend to the intelligible and to the existing offers difficulties in our human situation.

If we consider our intellectual knowledge we have a certain knowledge of physical natures. However presented as existents we know them only through sensible existence. This immediately involves the sense appetite, and the rational appetite, to reach them as existents, would have to be channelled back through sense appetite. This would involve consideration of the intellectual object under the aspect or *ratio* of suitability or non-suitability. And this does not offer any possibility of obtaining a transcendental notion of the good.

Now if we consider the quiddities as intellectual objects, natures as natures, and not just as physical natures can we not see everything that is, as a quiddity, not necessarily considering it as a particular quiddity of this or that kind, but just as quiddity? Can our appetite not tend to these quiddities as objects to be desired? But what exactly are we saying here? In speaking of all natures, there is implied a transcending of physical natures; a recognition that there are other beings than physical beings. Are we not saying that since we don't perceive them directly, that each, to be being, must have an essence or nature? Thus, to see the transcendental character of quiddity or essence, you really recognize a vague unity of all beings as being.

Essence, as a transcendental notion, implies the act of "to be," the aspect under which all are being. It is as if you explicitly see all natures or essences, each as the essence of a being, something that *is* or could be. In other words a plurality of essences can be reduced to a unity implied in all essences, as essences only by transcending the particular and reaching some common point of view. This cannot be a genus. One gets the more universal notion of being from the act of "to be," or in seeing all essences as essences of being. Having reached the analogical unity of being you have a certain unity of all essences, but this arises from the fact that they are seen as beings.

But the important point here is that if you consider natures or quiddities or essences as true of all being and not just as expressing physical natures, you really are recognizing being as beings and you have existence restored to these quiddities. In other words we are back in the field of reality and not just of knowledge.

Now reason can distinguish between a thing and its aspect of desirability. The aspect of desirability or the *ratio* is always the recognition of some actuality in the thing that in its own actuality is able to be perfective, either in the fashion of joining, typical of the physical order, or as tasted or fulfilling sense appetite, as in the sensible order. The actuality is recognized as making being more fully to be.

In the intellectual knowledge of being intellect recognizes that all that is, is something, a quiddity that exists. This aspect of existence intellect cannot express quidditatively though it tends to so express it. As we have seen, "to be" is expressed as an intelligibility in the judgment. Both the quidditative aspect and the existential aspect of being are understood by intellect as act. "To be" is recognized as the act of all acts even of forms. It is the act of essence which is seen like a formal perfection

yet different.[39] Both of these intelligibilities
can be seen as acts as perfective of intellect, considered according to the *ratio* of
the species, and as acts perfective of intellect, the will can tend to them as good but
note—it is as good for intellect. As intelligible, they are the object of intellect and
the existing perfection is the existence of
truth not of things as existing. It is rela-
tively easy to see all being as good from
this angle. And it is possible to stop there
because, for us, it is so easy to reduce or
think of intellectual knowledge of existence in a quidditative fashion. We also
tend to stop there because intellect in its
object, being, covers all being, and its
good, the true, is a transcendental. But the
truth of being as something existing is that
being is primary; it is "is" that is intelligible not the intelligible that is.

Reflecting we can see that if intellect
sees being as being and existence as the
act of all acts it knows being as it is in
itself—not just as known or on the level of

knowing, not first in its intentional existence, but with the actuality that gives it
an absolute, necessary character and position in as much as it is; with the actuality
that makes it itself and not other, tending
to the unique as it tends to the fulness of
being; with the actuality that constitutes
it as having an intelligible character tending in the fulness of being to be an intellect in act; this actuality recognized as the
completion of being, of what it is "to be,"
to exist is seen as perfective, and as the
perfection of being it specifies an intellectual appetite to tend to *esse ipsius,* the desire of being as being that is, as existent.[31]

In other words, intellect can understand the significance of act and the ultimate character of the act of existence. It
recognizes existence not only as a principle of a thing but as the primary constitut-
ing principle. It recognizes that existence
as such is prior to its knowing, or as the
existentialists say it is there. It recognizes
that beyond existence, there is nothing;

that no being is being without the act of existence; that if it, as a knowing being, is not complete, there is nothing but the existential that can complete it. So being, as an existent, is that which has value beyond all value. Intellect knows it is there but an intellectual being tends to assimilate it as intelligible. Thus intellect knowing apprehends being, as actuality; intellectual knowledge acts as the sight and evaluator of the *esse* that can perfect appetite. It cannot but present it to appetite except as that toward which it should tend. It presents actuality of being as existence to will as its end. Being actuates will as such an end. The actuality of existence pulls the will toward it as giving the will being, moving the will to join its actuality; moving the will to be more fully being through the act of love.

Thus there is a certain difficulty in saying that intellect apprehends the good. I think what is meant is that it apprehends the actuality of being and its significance and presents this to the will as its end. It puts in will, when specifying it, this fulness of being and in that sense moves it; makes it more to be, in that the will is made active to reach it.[32] The will's activity which results from an end as specifying it makes will an agent to reach the end. We can also consider the situation as the actuality of being in its own existence which when presented to the will pulls it to its "to be," and thus actuates the will. But the activity of the will, its love, is to love the thing not just as perfecting it but as perfection; as it is in itself. Being as *bonum* is the full flower of *ens*.

Is not this what St. Thomas means when he accepts the phrase the "good diffuses itself"[33] and then says this diffusion must be understood not as implying the operation of an efficient cause but that of a final cause? Being as diffusive, as good, fulfills and perfects as such. Will is attracted, is moved and fulfilled by it. In this diffusiveness as final causality consists the *ratio* of the good, that is, being as perfecting, seen as completing in its actuality. As it has this actuality in its mode of existence and as it is in itself perfect and so good, will as agent loves it. Thus all that is, in as much as it is, is good. The transcendental notion is not fully grasped except by intellect's reflection on the actualization of the will by the good as good and will's love of it. The transcendental notion is founded by a reflection on man's fullest and highest actualization which informs intellect of being's power to so pull and actualize.

Being as good, though it is *good for* any being that is not being itself, is yet intellectually understood and loved as it is, that is *good in itself*. Being as being is seen not only as perfective, for from that angle it becomes the perfecting object of some power, but it is also seen as perfection, as source and condition of all lower or lesser meanings of the good. But the good as good is primarily loved with a love that is in and for the good itself. As the love of being as existent it is love of that which is sufficient in itself; vaguely it is love of what makes a thing to be which ultimately is Existence Itself. Also vaguely Pure Existence is loved in and for itself. Thus the intellectual appetite naturally, though not clearly, tends to Pure Existence in tending to being intellectually understood in all things that are. At present we grasp existence only as we find being in the analogical unity of all the particular beings we know. From being in general arises the love of the good in general.[34] But within this love no particular being pulls the love of will with an absolutely necessitating pull.[35] Only being in its fulness can absolutely attract the love of will yet every being bespeaks being; each is an epiphany of it. Thus we necessarily love all that is in as much as it is, but in the field of being and the good only choice can fix the will.

St. Thomas marks very clearly the connection between *esse* or act of "to be" and the notion of the good when he says that the notion of number and line are considered by the mathematician not according as they are a physical number and line but only according to the *ratio* of the species or according as they are intelligible conceptions. And the good, he says, does not follow upon consideration of the *ratio* of the species or in as much as we consider an intelligible conception as such.[36] Such conceptions can only be seen as good as having existence in the mind but this is not strictly their being as they exist. Thus truth has not immediately the *ratio* of the good. As we said above, quiddities as quiddities or truth as truth cannot give us the transcendental notion of the good. Yet very often the idea of nature, or of truth as good rather than the existent is what is stressed in many treatises of the good. St. Augustine in his *De Natura Boni*[37] emphasizes this idea of nature or true as good. All things, he holds, are spirits or bodies; all vary in perfection or vary in their mode, species and order. There is a hierarchy of natures of greater or lesser degrees of intelligible form. And he stresses this hierarchy as established according to degrees of intelligibility. This hierarchy is, but it is only as a hierarchy of intelligible existences that it is good. To consider natures is to look at being as an object of intellect and so as the good of intellect, or the good of truth.

This point of view is almost natural for us, as we have said, because intellectual appetite tends to follow the first intellectual knowledge which is quidditative and this in its intellectual mode is not immediately existential. It is of course a position that identifies truth with being or speaks of being solely in terms of truth but in such a position, as it was pointed out, there is no explicit explanation of how you get to a transcendental notion or to the unifying of the plurality of truths, quiddities or essences.

To establish the hierarchy of good things, after the good is seen to be interchangeable with being, is a necessary step in marking the richness of the notion of the good. The good is an analogical notion and the richness of its diversity is just as important as its notion of unity, in order to show us more fully the richness of being.

Having shown how we come to a realization of the transcendental notion of the good let us note again that the order of the transcendentals is important for St. Thomas.[38] That is, he insists on this order if one considers the transcendental names in themselves. Considering the metaphysical meaning due to a developing reflection on being we see the metaphysical meanings of the properties or manifestations of being to be in the order of *ens, unum, verum, bonum.* What he is stressing is that in understanding being as being which takes into account the experience from which we abstract the intelligible significance, we slowly come to realize that everything that is, is an existing nature, that is, is itself and not another, a sort of unity, that only a unity can be intelligible and that in understanding being and unity we thus understand being is intelligible.

The intelligibility of being, understood as developing from *ens* and *unum*, together with an appreciation of the appetitive non-knowledge factor and its relation to being, brings us to an affirmation or evaluation of being as act. It brings us to an appreciation especially of the act of existence which act cannot be reduced to a quidditative status. The being actual in its own existence, is perfective, as we have seen, of appetite on the lower levels and on the intelligible level as an existent offers a rest to intellectual appetite. If this understood *esse* constitutes the *ratio* of the good, then only at the point at which being is seized as being that is, is seized not only as *ens*, but as a unity, and a unity that is intelligible, and the intelligible unity is seen as existing in its own reality, through its own act of existence, *does the good actuate strictly as good*. It is only where

being is seen in its absolute character that
the appetite in its act can love not only
what is *good for* it but love goodness in
itself. Here in this highest act of will it
loves being as it is, that is as being which
means being vaguely grasped in its total
perfection. The good is not good solely because it perfects or fills appetite; it is good
because it is, and actuality is perfection.
This perfection is primary to the secondary role of perfecting. Being, loved in this
primary fashion, stands as a metaphysical
basis for charity.

Moreover there seem to be two mo-
ments in respect to the transcendental notion of the true. One moment sees being
as intelligible; the other sees it in a fuller
sense of its relation as knowledge to appetite. When this non-knowledge factor is
included in the knowledge of being we intellectually appreciate, as has been shown,
the significance of being, the importance
of act as perfective of being and also the
perfection of being. This is the good as

apprehended or rather it is being's significance apprehended whereas that which is
proposed to will, is lovable and loved.

Maritain in his *Neuf Leçons sur les notions premières de la philosophie morale*
says: "Besides let us note that in a philosophy of realism the notion of value is not
reserved to a moral philosophy but has al-
ready and, in the first instance, its place in
a speculative philosophy. It is because the
notion of value is a valid and legitimate
notion in metaphysics that we can understand that it is legitimate and necessary in
ethics."[39]

Where then is the metaphysical basis
of the notion of moral value if not in connection with the metaphysical notion of
the good? And what aspect of it could one
consider as value if not this understood
significance of being which is to specify
the will? Thus one could say that intellect
evaluates being, and sees that being has
value in itself and proposed to the will is
what will in its act or exercise loves and

in which it rests as the good. In an essentialist philosophy the notion of value would predominate both in metaphysics and ethics; it would bespeak an identification of being with truth and so the good with the good of truth. It would neglect the good of actual existence which, as we have tried to show, is the meaning of *bonum* emphasized in an existentialist philosophy. An existentialist philosophy would distinguish the notion of truth of being, its intelligibility from its aspect of having value. The value aspect is that which specifies the will but is still the truth of the good, whereas the transcendental notion of the good would have in it added to the notion of value, an appreciation of being as actually loved and so lovable by will. It is being as loved or lovable that is expressed in *bonum*.

Will, tending toward being in as much as it exists, is tending to everything in as much as it is an expression of being and this is vaguely to tend to being as Pure

Act, a being whose essence is Existence. However, the concrete mode of existence is not given; there is only given to our will immediately the universe of being, each thing vaguely in as much as it is being, and together with this the law that being to be must be being.

Through the ways of causality the existence of God can be proved. He will be seen as the First Cause of being; He who is; His essence is "to be." He is Pure Act in its highest form; He is one, unique, the true in perfect actuality. He is the understood in act and understanding in act, perfectly fused to be in His essence an intellectual act of perfect Intelligibility which begets a love of that perfect intelligible existence itself and so is most interior to it. He is a unique act of pure intelligible love of existence. What must be remembered is that intellect judges that the first cause is such. In other words that He is one, true, and good since He is the cause of things that actually exist as one, true, and good. But the manner of existence of that which is Existence Itself absolutely transcends any modes understood by us. That mode is something we cannot comprehend; in other words we judge that He is and is so but we cannot seize in judgment the exact manner in which that perfect mode of existence exists.

However seeing God as Cause of being it is manifest that that perfection of all perfection—"to be," is His perfect effect. Also those aspects of being which slowly unfold as new visions such as unity, truth, and goodness depend directly on Him, Pure Is, as Unique, as Pure Act of Intelligence and Pure Act of Love; then He is explicitly seen as the ultimate basis of the transcendental n o t i o n of the true and good. It is at this point that one can speak of the true as related to God's intellect, and the good as a notion dependent on His will. But these transcendental notions are to a degree intelligible and definable without immediate reference to their relation to God. Otherwise we could not use them to prove in a metaphysical fashion, God as pure Existence.

But to return to the notion of the good, St. Thomas says that God is of His essence good or Goodness Itself because He is *Ipsum Esse.*[40] Thus he emphasizes that the principle by which beings participate in existence is the principle of their goodness. But those things whose essence is not existence are good but not the essence of goodness. Thus, looking back again, it is clearer that if intellect considers being in as much as it is being, that is, in as much as it is actual with the highest act, the intellectual appetite will tend toward existence. But this appetite, the will, tends toward a concrete; it will vaguely seek a being that is being, or existence Itself.

But such an object, we repeat, is not given in the transcendental notion of being as being. Will so specified can tend only to goodness in general, and even with the proof of the existence of God the situation is not resolved. Intellect can understand that God is Being Itself, and its ultimate object is to comprehend Him. And, if the intellect c o u l d comprehend Him, will would have the object in which it could rest.[41] But intellect comprehends Him only through His effects and so will tends toward Him but is not given the concrete existence that will elicit a definite act of love that is stable and undeviating. Rather it rests only in the actual that is actually possessed. Yet, it is evident, will's good is to love in a most existential fashion.

Before we can go on to solve the difficulty of the will and its object and so the further development of the meaning of the good, we must consider another characteristic of being as it is immediately known by us.

St. Thomas points out many times that no finite being is its own operation.[42] For example, to know and to will is to be in act, and if this act were the being's substance, the substance would be just this act of knowing, it couldn't have potentiality to know, for it is a contradiction to be and to be potential at the same time. He Whose *esse* is identical with His *agere* would have to be a unique action and this would be God.

In all creatures, the act of "to be" is considered the primary act and the act of operation, or "to act" is the secondary act. The operation as a power in the thing is a potency having its roots in the existing essence. This operation is not accidental as being added to the substance but rather that substance being the kind it is, gives rise to these powers. So the existing essence is the source of the power to act. The operation is an act of a specified power when the power acts as an agent. Thus intellect is a power of the soul. Its object is being, and the soul in the act of knowing can become, in a sense, all being. Also intellectual appetite or will is a power which, specified by intellect, and so informed can operate, and tend to, and love being. Yet this union of the intellectual being with being through the soul's operations does not beget the pure identity of Pure Act. The act of *esse* is the source of the act but never identical with the act of *agere*. Thus St. Thomas can say that when a thing is, it is good though not absolutely but *"secundum quid."*[43] But a being that is and is developed through activity as having reached its end, is good absolutely. This stresses again that goodness results from the actuality of a thing and that, He is Goodness Itself or Goodness Absolutely in Whom *esse* and *agere* are identical.[44]

"To be" then for a finite being is to be and to act. To be isn't a sort of static positing, but rather "to be" is to be a source of activity and, with the help of other things, to be actually in act. Therefore no being as being and as finite is unrelated. And the fundamental ontological order of the universe flows from the nature of created beings as actual existing sources of activity. Yet it is also true that the order of the world (its actual relations) is not entirely readable in the nature of things because these natures, as essences partially potential, give rise to various possible relations; secondly, there are in fact chance events arising not only from such essences but from the very multiplicity of caused events, which bring about the chance occurence but are not explainable through the activity of each cause separately understood;[45] thirdly, there are beings whose natures is to be the lord of their act; beings who choose so to act. This last is an order caused by free agents and is freely caused.[46]

To be good is not only "to be" but "to act" and so to be more fully according to its activity. By its secondary act the finite being shares in the totality of being, for example, the good of the totality of the physical world.

There is thus the good of "to be" and the good or actuality of "to act." This latter belongs not to the substantial being but to the order of the relation of substances, yet through this order there is brought an added good, that of the whole.

In considering the transcendental notion of unity we noted that "to be" is also to be one, and that this notion of unity was included in the evaluation of being and so formed part of the significance of the good. Thus will tends to that which is one. The love of the good in general is love of being, not in its plurality, but in as much as each of the many is an expression of being. It is love of "is" in as much as it is an expression of Unique Being though this is only vaguely understood in the analogical notion. The universe of being stressed in the notion of unity through relatedness, shows forth the whole as good in that it is seen as variegated vision of the perfection of being, yet never attaining to that perfect unity of the Unique.

But it is in regard to intellectual being endowed with free will that the good takes on an even more special meaning for man.

As lord of his acts he to a degree establishes a relation and order in being. His action as a rational and voluntary being can affect, to a degree, the order of being in the universe, and so aid or not aid being in its effort to be. However his action as a primarily immanent action causes the rational subject to be, and in a sense to be the fulness of being within himself, rather than to be the totality of being through relation of one part, or one unit to another. The spiritual action of knowing and desiring and choosing is not just a joining with other beings but a union and identification with being as other and so is an assimilation of the total perfection of being. Man is, but he is not fully, except through his operation which as spiritual and immanent is the assimilation of the total perfection of being as perfective of him, and the total fulness of being as loved by him as being, therefore loved in itself and more than himself.

This particular *"agere"* of man, man as master of his acts, establishes a certain order, a union of being and so completeness and goodness. Thus it must be considered in order to see the relation of moral and ontological good. For every finite being, "to be" and "to act," is to be fully and so be good absolutely; it is to be ontologically good together with that goodness completed, by this moral goodness which flows not just from his ontological good but from the act of his choice. This close connection of ontological goodness and man's responsibility in the accomplishment of his moral goodness points in man to a possibility of an ontological lack or privation should man fail. More positively, from facts as they are known, it points to an ontological gift should man act as he can and should.

Metaphysics and ethics are often not very closely related in expositions of Aristotelian and Thomistic philosophy and thus the relations of the ontological and moral good are not made very clear.

Aristotle sees man as a complex being whose *"agere"* is not simple. Man seeks happiness but in analyzing this Aristotle sees that man seeks a certain prosperity as regards external goods; he also seeks virtue and its happiness and also contemplation of the highest truths and its happiness.[47] Is there a hierarchy of ends? What is the principle of unification, or does he seek one?

According to one of the latest interpretations of his metaphysics it would seem that Wisdom as contemplation is a "knowing of knowing."[48] This knowing is the knowing of form as act, as an intelligible content which has "finitude, necessity and determination."[49] The unity of forms is only that arising from science of forms.[50]

Aristotle is his *Ethics* indicates clearly that intellectual contemplation of the highest truth is that which is good in itself and not in view of something else. Moreover he makes clear each man has this contemplation of the highest truth and happiness only in the measure that reason is the end of the lower faculties. Also this knowing or contemplating of the highest truths is the best possible life, so it is the good. And since Aristotle maintains "that the good investigated in its innermost nature by Wisdom is the same good which dominates the practical order;"[51] and if man can reach to this knowing of knowing typical of Separate Entities only in so far as they are reflected in sensible things,[52] it seems natural that Aristotle should stress the prudential life of virtue and its happiness or the good on that level. But does that mean that virtue and its happiness does not contain in any sense the contemplation of form?

Père Deman in his work on Prudence points out that Aristotle does not consider that prudence which rules the life of virtue ought to or does consult Wisdom and its principles.[53] Rather he notes the Aristotelian distinction of the two orders of life and the happiness concomitant to each: the first order that of contemplation, and the other that of acting well. Professor Bourke says "Aristotle's man looks only to subjective self-perfection."[54] At least we should be warned against indicating too readily a close parallelism between Ethics and Metaphysics in the philosophy of Aristotle and that of St. Thomas. A metaphysics of a plurality of forms will not have the same unity as a metaphysics of existence. And this difference is reflected on the manner of unifying or relating the ontological and moral good.

Let us consider St. Thomas. Père Deman declares that St. Thomas, unlike Aristotle, does connect prudence with the principles of intelligence but these are the principles of practical intellect. But, like Aristotle, he considers that practical science is other than speculative science. Moreover he holds that for St. Thomas moral virtues with which prudence is connected have no need of intellectual virtues such as wisdom and science though prudence has need of intelligence, that is, it must refer to the first principles of practical reason. Thus ethics is not a deduction starting from metaphysics nor does it presuppose conclusions of metaphysics. St. Thomas, he holds, strongly affirms the distinction, or rather the separation, of the the practical and speculative order.[55]

Certainly one does not have to develop the conclusion of metaphysics in order to have the first principles of ethics. That is really supposing the impossible considering the urgent demands of action. The fundamental, simple directive of action must be as immediate and evident as the fundamental intelligibility of being in terms of which we express all intelligibilities. This fundamental directive must follow the same order of levels as the knowledge of being. To be intelligent does not demand the full development of the science of metaphysics as a science; nor does to be moral demand either the development of metaphysical science or even of ethical science as such. But the philosopher as scientist, especially as a metaphysician, is definitely interested in asking in what sense one can speak of two definite sets of principles, one of the speculative order and the other of the practical order. Or the same problem put another way: how does one speak of *bonum* as both ontological and moral, calling them both good?

Before trying to resolve this connection we might note that from the supernatural point of view St. Thomas does not stress the distinction of the speculative and practical order, but rather the influence of one on the other.[56]

Knowledge of God's being given through faith and the supernatural gifts affecting intellect in its understanding in a speculative fashion, are also immediately regulative of practical knowledge. So that which is speculative in this order is also immediately practical.

Why this difference of the two orders? Is the situation of the natural order one in which speculative and practical are absolutely distinct while the situation of the supernatural order is one in which they tend to identity?

First of all, the intellect as speculative, taking apprehension in a broad sense, apprehends the truth of things. It has as its object the true, and this can include the good as intelligible and it can therefore include the will whose object is an end or a good. So the intellect is not considered practical just because it has in it some consideration of the good, but the intellect is practical in as much as what it apprehends it apprehends as directive of something to be done. The intellect as practical is thus directive of something to be done. As practical it is directive or causative. But is it not the good desired that makes intellect so use or so formulate from what it knows, a principle directive of action? Or, as St. Thomas says, *"objectum intellectus est bonum ordinabile ad opus sub ratione veri."*[57] As intellect, its object is the true but it is intellect moved to consider something to be done, and this movement is from will desiring the good. Thus the intellect under the influence or pull of the good considers the true as a means or a principle directive of doing.

Here we are considering the intellect as practical with respect to the order of man's voluntary acts—or man's moral work.

Now knowledge given in faith is, from one aspect, in as much as faith is a virtue of intellect, concerned with truth, the truth about the Being of God, as He is in Himself accepted on the word of God. It is God, given as He actually exists, not just as cause of things existing. As such it is like knowledge of an existent and, more than that, it is knowledge of Perfect Existence, and so the highest speculative knowledge.[58]

But also faith operates through love. It is an act of will that maintains the intellectual assent and it is love that increases the insight of faith.[59] Thus God is seen as an object of knowledge, the truth of His

Goodness that can be loved, but He is more given to love or charity than even to knowledge—for He is given as end to be hoped for as seen. Faith is also an act of will, the result of choice so He is loved as the Highest Good. What is given in faith is a speculative knowledge of the Highest Good that is maintained through the impulsion of the will. So it can also be seen as practical knowledge, knowledge concerning the end that the will desires and the way it should be desired. Thus knowledge given in faith as a speculative principle is also immediately a principle of the practical order, because the First Truth is the Ultimate End. From the natural point of view, speculative knowledge is not so immediately directive of the practical order of action. Primarily because of a difference in the character of the knowledge and also as intellectual it is general, about being in general, and the good in general.[60] While action is concerned with the concrete, with the immediate existential mode as it is able to be ordered or grasped by us in a singular, concrete act. Because then of the different conditions of existence there is a possibility of speaking of these two orders separately. Moreover, as we have seen, "to be" and "to act" are not identical in a finite being. There is a development of being through good operation but there is always the primacy of *esse* to *agere*. Thus knowledge that has to do with the *esse* of things, what they necessarily are in as much as they are, is not the same as the knowledge dealing with action, especially practical action that is in our power and is contingent.

Considering the speculative order, intellect in its highest knowledge seizes being as being and evaluates its actuality and thus specifies the will which is pulled to this actuality as good. This knowledge of being is analogical and so the will tends to the good as analogical, or the good in general. Intellect can appreciate the truth of this good, and from this it so forms the

transcendental notion of the good. Such
an analogical notion, as general, does not
move to action immediately; it is not immediately directive of work which has to
do ultimately with the particular sensible
concrete. It is only the particular concrete,
in as much as it is actual and good, that
moves to a definite concrete action concerning a concrete situation.

Thus man is in the position in which
his appetite tends to existence as good, but
he experiences only particular existents.
He can, through reasoning, know that
God, Pure Existence, is the object he
should seek but He is not so given in His
own existence that He necessarily actuates
the will. Therefore being as being and
the principles connected with it, or the
highest speculative knowledge of being as
good, are not immediately principles of
operation. Such a consideration of operation will be brought about only when the
end is a concrete good, when the *ratio* of
the good is identical with, or, from some

aspect, is identified with an existent of this order.

On the other hand an absolute disconnectedness of these orders, speculative and practical, their notions and principles does not seem to be according to the mind of St. Thomas.

First of all this is seen from the position we have noted regarding "to be" and "to act." To be makes a thing good *"secundum quid"* but to act makes a thing good absolutely. This bespeaks a close connection between the *esse* and the operation, so knowledge concerned with *esse* cannot be knowledge unconnected with knowledge dealing with operation. For one could not then intelligently perfect his being.

Secondly, speaking of the goodness and evil of human acts St. Thomas stresses as a basic notion the convertibility of *ens* and *bonum* and says the human act is good when it has the *"esse"* it ought to have, that it is the ontological actuality or being it ought to have.[61] So in explaining the moral

good it seems impossible to ignore the meaning of the good in metaphysics.

But how exactly is the good in its speculative, metaphysical meaning incorporated into the notion of moral goodness?

The problem is to guard the primacy of the notion of good in the ontological order and yet see that the notion of the good is a first principle, not a derived one, in the order of human action. Yet in some sense as belonging to the order of operation, the moral good, absolutely speaking is subordinate to the good ontologically considered.

Let us see if we can bring these two notions together. In going through the transcendental notions we saw that being is, is one, is true. Also being was seen at all its different levels in its actuality as perfective of being. And intellect appreciating being not only as intelligible but also in its existential actuality as end of inclination or appetite has an apprehension of value or of the significance of being as being which it presents to its intellectual appetite, and this as end, draws the will to it as the good. But as this is the good in general man's intellectual appetite is pulled to love, but is neither satisfied nor fixed because of the lack of a concrete existential mode. The will, aroused but not satisfied, reacts immediately on the power, the intellect which specifies it, and moves intellect in a general fashion. The will awakens, as it were, intellect to consider how it could be practical to investigate means or ways for the satisfaction and fixation of intellectual appetite. Intellect and will as two powers of the one spiritual soul have a reciprocal causality that is immediate and intimate.

The moment intellect is moved by the will it looks at things in the light of the good.[62] In this light the intellect seeks to understand the good in the light of the good. Moreover it understands that to fulfil the will it must be definite as regards the end. Now we may ask what is the general character of the principle that will regulate such action, that is the general principle that must impregnate the movement of intellect as practical? It must be an intellectual principle and so in some sense affirm being, but it must be a principle concerning the good because it is about the good that intellect is thinking. It must be a principle that affirms the good. The good must be. In this program intellect is really making its guiding principle this: that the good must be and that all ways to the good or end must affirm it and not contradict it. Do good. Do what makes the end be. Thus means would be brought under the light of the end; they are affirmed as good. Any thing that would contradict the good or end would be evil and should not be done. Thus the first principle of the practical order so enunciated is as immediate as the principle of identity. It is the intellect affirming the first principle of being when moved by the good and affirming it in terms of the good. But it is yet too general a principle. It is almost speculative, but yet is practical since intellect is under the impulsion of the good to consider the principle of achieving the good.

The situation would be that simple and such would be the sole and immediate connection of the metaphysical and moral good if man's situation were simple and solely intellectual and if the good or end were seen in a sufficiently concrete fashion to move to the deliberation of means, not in general but in the concrete. But actually intellect is aroused only in a very vague and general way to consider the good. For in the natural order the perfect, ontological good, Pure Existence, is not given as the good exerting the pull. Thus it is not that good that is immediately moving intellect to investigate means of seeking it more fully or loving it.

The good in general actuating the will but not satisfying it because it is general, does rouse intellect to be interested in the good in the fashion mentioned. Intellect, however, also sees that it must resolve the situation according to the conditions as they are, for the concrete good lies in the actual existent. At this point under the general influence of being, in as much as it is good, intellect decides on a particular being that is good and that can be a definite end. Since reason can investigate God as First Cause and see Him as a spiritual being it can also see He should be the end of man's highest powers, intellect and will, and that as First Cause He must also be the Ultimate End. In the light of his reasoning man can choose God as his end. This choice would fix a definite end within the general notion of the good in general. And in the light of this end the intellect would seek practical means to seek it. With this choice the first principle then: Do good; would be: do what is a means to your last end; and this would be God. It would affirm the being of God as embodying the highest principle of being, highest perfection of being, the Good.

Yet, in the natural order, God is not given as end except in so far as reason can see that the first cause should be the last end; God transcends man's power to reach Him as an existent. Actually then in the existential order, among goods that are given, man must choose an end that would, as it were, face the right way. As St. Thomas says man may lack the power or means for obtaining perfect beatitude yet he is not lacking in what is necessary for him to reach his end. For free choice is given to man by which he is able to turn to God Who would make him happy. For as Aristotle says in his *Ethics,* "what is possible through friends we are able to do in some manner through ourselves."[63]

Or even lacking a clear proof of the existence of God man actuated by the good as good can investigate the actual good within his reach. Through reflection on himself knowing and desiring he can see the intellectual powers as dominating the others. Their objects may be too universal

to determine action but man can see himself as specifically man through these
powers and the objects of these powers
as embodying the deepest significance of
being. So to use the concrete beings and
things suitable to him in such a way as to
maintain himself as man, is in any concrete
situation to act rationally. Man uses things
suitable to his various inclinations in such
a way as to develop himself as man. This
brings all things, in as much as man can
bring them under the object of his intellect
and will. He would choose as an end
therefore that which would best maintain
him as an intellectual being dependent on
sensible knowledge and needing to a degree to fulfill in a concrete situation both
sense and intellectual appetite. Such an
end would not be ultimate but, as affirming this particular thing suitable to man in
this situation, it would be placed under the
ratio of the good as the good which is
proper to his intellectual power. He would

have an end then that would be a means
to the ultimate.

If we now consider the first principle:
Do good and avoid evil: we might say it
means act rationally. But to act rationally
is to affirm the object of intellect and its
intellectual appetite, so it is still an affirmation of being and the good as object of
these highest powers. But it is not a direct
affirmation. Rather it is an affirmation of
this particular existent, suitable to this or
that appetite of man but so desired as to
maintain him as a rational being, in the
existential situation in which he finds himself. Ultimately so considered it is taken
as a temporary end, as a means, and is seen
only as something suitable to man's highest
powers. But the objects of his highest
powers to the degree that they are envis-
aged in their own right are objective. In
the object intellectually understood the
good is seen not just as that which is suitable to man as rational being, though it
must be so seen, but also the object is seen

as it is, something that is being, intelligible, actual, and that has in itself an intrinsic character which maintains being to be, and so good. St. Thomas stresses, I think, that man must have a certain awe of existence, even of those modes below his.

The moral good always presupposes the ontological, metaphysical notion of the good but man, a complex being in a concrete, complex situation is not living a purely spiritual life. Everything may have an intelligible aspect but it also has the aspect of "suitable to some power." Man with his various powers and appetites must evaluate being not just intellectually as expressed in its ultimate act of existence and in itself but in the rich diversitiy or modes of being that being exemplifies and in their variegated relations to him. Man does not live as just an intellect but to be an intellect he must understand himself and his approaches to the richness of being in all its manifestations of existence. Thus he must face the rich diversity of the modes of being, construct a hierarchy and a hierarchy in reference to his nature especially with respect to his intellectual powers so that through that nature he may assimilate being itself. Thus the ontological good in reference to the maintenance of man as rational constitutes the basis of moral goodness.[64] But the more the intellect of man is developed the more will he be disturbed by this making of the ontological good as being, a means or a thing subordinated to him as man, even as rational. Being as being he can see as good in itself and he will tend to the perfection of being as his end. The moral good and the ontological as ultimate end coincide.

The ideal then, for man, would be that condition in which the end, Pure Existence, could be present to man as an Existent, and more than this that it could be present even in a manner in accord with his mode of sensitive, intelligent existence. In such a case the highest ontological good would also be given as an end that could be directly and immediately man's end, and no means would play the role of end. Man's moral good would then immediately coincide with the highest ontological good. Naturally speaking it seems an impossibility. But if, through Revelation, it is so given we can realize how suitable it is; we can see the need of faith perfecting intellect, and charity perfecting the will but we can also see how the needs of our nature are fused with, first the higher possibilities of intellect's openness on being, perfected in faith through the beginning of vision; and secondly, the higher possibilities of intellectual appetite or will seeking Pure Existence perfected by charity and seized through hope of vision. Moreover it seems most suitable if good is Incarnate in a person whose human nature can be connatural to the state of our human intellect and wills.[65] Thus, in this ideal condition, the Highest Truth as speculative is also seen as immediately practical because of the perfect fusion of the good of being and the good of man as a rational creature. The Incarnation stands as the good perfect for us which we love as It is in Itself, the Perfectly Good. It is the Good; It is given as good for us; and in the mystery of the Mystical Body we can in some manner be one with Him—and we can be absolutely good—Perfect as the Heavenly Father. But that is a great mystery.

NOTES

1. J. Maritain, *Les sept leçons sur l'être* (Paris Tequi, 1932-33), p. 78.
   —: *Neuf leçons sur les notions premières de la philosophie morale* (Paris, Tequi, 1949), p. 29. "La notion de bien est une notion première . . . qui surgit d'un coup, sous un certain angle de vision, pour révéler une nouvelle face de l'être, un nouveau mystère intelligible consubstantiel à l'être."

2. R. J. Henle, S.J., *Method in Metaphysics* (Aquinas Lecture, 1950, Marquette University Press, Milwaukee, 1951), p. 55.

3. *In Boetio de Trinitate*, q 6, a 2: "Principium igitur cujuslibet nostrae cognitionis est in sensu, quia ex apprehensione sensus oritur apprehensio phantasiae quae est motus a sensu factus . . . a qua iterum oritur apprehensio intellectivae animae ut objecta . . . Sed terminus cognitionis non semper est uniformiter: quandoque enim est in sensu, quandoque in imaginatione, quandoque in solo intellectu."

   Metaphysics has its origin in sense experience, as all knowledge has. But metaphysical knowledge is one expressed in intellectual judgments that terminate on being as rendered intelligible.

4. *De Veritate*, q 1, a 1; *Sum. Theol.*, I, q 5, a 1; q 16, a 3.

5. *Sum. Theol.*, I, q 16, a 4; q 16, a 4, ad 2.

6. This intelligibility of *ens, unum, verum* is explicitly seen when we elaborated explicitly the metaphysical notion of *bonum*.

7. *Sum. Theol.*, I, q 4, a 1, ad 3.

8. *Sum. Theol.*, I, q 11, a 1. ". . . inde est quod unumquodque, sicut custodit suum esse, ita custodit suam unitatem."

9. *Sum. Theol.*, I, q 16, a 3, ad 3.

10. G. Smith, S.J., *Natural Theology* (New York, Macmillan Co., 1951), p. 15: "There is no answer to the question, Why is being being? any more than there is an answer to the question Why is hot hot? All we can say to such pseudo-questions is to point out that just as it is the nature of the hot to be hot, so it is the nature of being to be."
Cf. also *In De Causis*, Lib. I, p. VI: "Probat autem Philosophus in IX Metaphysicorum, quod unumquodque cognoscitur per id quod

est in actu: et ideo ipsa actualitas rei est quoddam lumen ipsius."

11. Et. Gilson, *Wisdom and Love in St. Thomas Aquinas* (Marquette University Press, Milwaukee, 1951), p. 24.

12. F. X. Maquart, *Elementa Philosophiae*, T. III, Metaphysica II (Paris, A. Blot, 1938), p. 116. He appears to demand this immediate reference to God in the definition of the transcendental *verum*.

13. J. Maritain, *Les sept leçons sur l'être*, p. 76.

14. *Cont. Gent.*, I, 38, 1. "Esse enim actu, in unoquoque est bonum ipsius; sed Deus non solum est ens actu, sed est Ipsum Suum Esse . . . Est igitur ipsa bonitas, non tantum bonus."

15. *Cont. Gent.*, I, 37, 3: "Omnia autem appetunt esse actu, secundum modum suum, quod patet ex hoc, quod unumquodque secundum naturam suam repugnat corruptioni. Esse igitur actu boni rationem constituit."
Cf. also *Cont. Gent.*, III, 3, 3.
Cont. Gent., III, 7, 2: "Unumquodque secundum suam essentiam habet esse. In quantum autem habet esse, habet aliquod bonum; nam si bonum est quod omnia

appetunt, oportet ipsum esse bonum dicere, quum omnia esse appetunt. Secundum hoc igitur unumquodque bonum est, quod essentiam habet."

16. *Sum. Theol.*, I-II, q 9, a 1, ad 2. "Sicut imaginatio formae sine aestimatione convenientis vel nocivi non movet appetitum sensitivum, ita nec apprehensio veri sine ratione boni et appetibilis movet appetitum intellectivum qui est voluntas. Unde intellectus speculativus non movet, sed intellectus practicus . . ."

17. *Sum. Theol.*, I-II, q 10, a 2. "Sicut autem coloratum in actu est objectum visus, ita bonum est objectum voluntatis. Unde, si proponatur aliquod objectum voluntati quod sit universaliter bonum et secundum omnem considerationem, ex necessitate voluntas in illud tendit, sed si aliquid velit; non enim poterit velle oppositum."

18. *Sum. Theol.*, I-II, q 9, a 2. "Id quod apprehenditur sub ratione boni et convenientis, movet voluntatem per modum objecti."

19. *De Veritate*, q 21, a 1.

20. *Ibid.*

21. *De Malo*, q 1, a 1. "Tertio idem apparet ex hoc quod ipsum esse maxime habet rationem appetibilis; unde videmus quod unumquodque naturaliter appetit conservare suum esse, et refugit destructiva sui esse, et eis pro posse resistit. Sic ergo ipsum esse, inquantum est appetibile, est bonum."

22. Et. Gilson, *L'esprit de la philosophie médiévale* (1ère series, Paris, Vrin, 1932), p. 91.

23. *De Veritate*, q 1, a 9.

24. *De Veritate*, q 25, a 1. "Nihil enim est aliud appetitus naturalis quam quaedam inclinatio rei, et ordo ad aliquam rem sibi convenientem . . ."

25. *Ibid.*

26. *Ibid.*

27. *Ibid.*

28. To generalize the aspect of suitability or non-suitability into a supposedly transcendental notion is merely to take a relative aspect of certain things to certain other things and generalize it under the concept of relative aspect. Such a concept is a being of the reason and the negation of metaphysics.

Cf. Bittle, *Domain of Being* (Bruce Publishing Co., Milwaukee, 1939). He says the intrinsic good for a being is its own nature. They "are good for the individuals who possess them . . ." p. 188. "And thus we may eventually define the good as any reality which suits the nature of the being which strives for it." p. 188. " 'Goodness' in the abstract would then be defined as the suitability of a reality for the nature of this being which strives for it." p. 189.

Cf. Glenn, *Ontology* (B. Herder Book Co., St. Louis, Mo., 1937). In speaking of the good he says, "There is a common character. It is this: a good thing answers a natural appetite, tendency, or desire." p. 155.

But he goes on to say that "every being (in as much as actual) is capable of answering a tendency, desire, or appetite . . . —Hence actual being, in as far as it is being at all is desirable or good." p. 156.

Here at least all are considered as being, i.e., as actual. But the good is seen solely in terms of *good for*, and as we have shown this differs in the physical, sensible and intellectual order. It is only when you see the good as good, that the *good for* is truly incorporated into the transcendental notion.

29. *Sum. Theol.*, I, q 19, a 1.

30. Cf. Note 7.

31. De Raeymaker, *La Philosophie de l'être: essai de synthèse métaphysique* (2 ed. rev. et corr., Louvain, Institut supèrieur de philosophie, 1947).

Certainly one is considering being as active when being is considered as knowing and desiring. M. De Raeymaker says, "Le bien transcendental concern donc formellement l'être actif." p. 249. It certainly concerns intellect appreciating will's love of existence and so appreciates what the actuality of "to be" means. But if I understand him correctly I do not agree that the good as good refers *primarily* to the act of the substantial form but rather to act as existence, or the actuality of substantial perfection. The substantial perfection in the analogical notion is there but indistinctly so as not to break the fragile unity.

M. De Raeymaker says, "Mais le "mode" selon lequel il possède la perfection d'être dépend de sa détermination quidditative, à savoir du principe de substantialité auquel le principe d'être est lié ou, selon l'expression consacrée 'dans lequel ce principe est reçu' et par lequel est individué. La *forme substantielle*, l'acte dans l'ordre de l'essence substantielle, détermine la perfection specifique de l'être particulier, elle fix la mesure de sa bonté naturelle et dès lors aussi le niveau et le rythme de son activité." p. 251.

Cf. also W. O'Connor, "The Nature of the Good," *Thought* (Fordham University Quarterly, Dec., 1949), pp. 639-655.

32. *De Veritate*, q 22, a 13.

33. *De Veritate*, q 21, a 1, ad 4. "dicendum quod 'diffundere' licet secundum proprietatem vocabuli videatur importare operationem causae efficientis, tamen largo modo potest importare habitudinem cujuscumque causae, sicut influere et facere, et alia hujusmodi. Cum autem dicitur quod bonum est diffusivum secundum sui rationem, non est intelligenda effusio secundum quod importat operationem causae efficientis, sed secundum quod importat habitudinem causae finalis; et talis diffusio non est mediante aliqua virtute superaddita. Dicit autem bonum diffusionem causae finalis, et non causae agentis, tum quia efficiens, inquantum hujusmodi, non est rei mensura et perfectio, sed magis initium; tum quia effectus, participat causam efficien-

tem secundum assimilationem formae tantum;
sed finem consequitur res secundum totum
esse suum, et in hoc consistebat ratio boni."

34. *De Malo*, q 1, a 4. "Intellectualis autem
natura sola apprehendit ipsam rationem boni
communem per intellectum, et in bonum
commune movetur per appetitum voluntatis."

35. *De Malo*, q 6, a 1. "Sed forma intellecta est
universalis sub qua multa possunt compre-
hendi; unde cum actus sint in singularibus in
quibus nullum est quod adaequat potentiam
universalis, remanet inclinatio voluntatis in-
determinate se habens ad multa."

36. *De Veritate*, q 21, a 2, ad 4. "Ipsum enim
esse lineae vel numeri bonum est, sed a
mathematico non considerantur secundum
suum esse, sed solum secundum rationem
speciei; considerat enim cum abstractione;
non enim sunt abstracta secundum esse, sed
solum secundum rationem. Dictum est autem
supra . . . quod bonum non sequitur rationem
speciei nisi secundum esse quod habet in re
aliqua; et ideo ratio boni non competit lineae
vel numero secundum hoc quod cadunt in
consideratione mathematica, quamvis linea et
numerus bona sint."

37. *Oeuvres de Saint Augustin,* Ire série: Opuscules I, La Morale Chrétienne — De Natura Boni. (Texte de l'Édition Bénédictine, Paris, Desclée de Brouwer & Cie, 1949), pp. 440-509.

38. *De Veritate,* q 21, a 3. "Unde istorum nominum transcendentium talis est ordo, si secundum se considerantur; quod post ens est unum, deinde verum, deinde post verum bonum."

39. J. Maritain, *Neuf leçons sur les notions premières de la philosophie morale,* p. 20.

40. *Cont. Gent.,* I, 38, 1. "Esse enim actu, in unoquoque est bonum ipsius; sed Deus non solum est ens actu, sed est Ipsum Suum Esse . . . Est igitur Ipsa Bonitas, non tantum bonus."

41. *De Malo,* q 3, a 3. "Bonum autem perfectum, quod est Deus, necessariam quidem connexionem habet cum beatitudine hominis, quia sine eo non potest homo esse beatus; verumtamen necessitas hujus connexionis non manifeste apparet homini in hac vita, quia Deum per essentiam non videt; et ideo etiam voluntas hominis in hac vita non ex necessitate Deus adhaerit;"

42. *Sum. Theol.*, I, q 54, a 1.

43. *Sum. Theol.*, I, q 5, a 1, ad 1.

44. *Sum. Theol.*, I, q 14, a 4.

45. Smith, *Natural Theology*, pp. 148, 149, 150.

46. *Sum. Theol.*, I-II, q 1, a 1.

47. Aristotle, *Nicomachean Ethics*, The Basic Works of Aristotle (ed. Richard McKeon, New York, Random House, 1941), Bk. X. Cf. also J. Leonard, S.J., *Le Bonheur chez Aristote* (Bruxelles, 1948) for various types of life and happiness connected with them.

48. J. Owens, C.Ss.R., *The Doctrine of Being in the Aristotelian Metaphysics* (Toronto, Pontifical Institute of Mediaeval Studies, 1951), p. 296.

49. *Ibid.*, p. 296.

50. *Ibid.*, p. 297.

51. *Ibid.*, p. 85.

52. *Ibid.*, p. 296.

53. T. H. Deman, O.P., *Saint Thomas d'Aquin, Somme Théologique, La Prudence* — Appendice II, Renseigments Techniques (Paris, Desclée & Cie, 1949), p. 420.

54. V. Bourke, in his *St. Thomas and the Greek Moralists* (Marquette University Press, Mil-

waukee, 1947) says, "There is completely
lacking, in the original Aristotelianism, the
ordering of free human acts to an objectively
real, ultimate end. Aristotle's man looks only
to subjective self-perfection; his God has
nothing to do with human acts."

55. Deman, *op. cit.*, pp. 444-445.

56. *Ibid.*, pp. 445-446.

57. *Sum. Theol.*, I, q 79, a 11, ad 2.

58. *Sum. Theol.*, II-II, q 1, a 1. ". . . si consid-
eremus formalem rationem objecti, nihil est
aliud quam veritas prima."
Sum. Theol., II-II, q 4, a 2. "Credere autem
est immediate actus intellectus, quia objectum
hujus actus est verum, quod proprie pertinet
ad intellectum."
Sum. Theol., II-II, q 4, a 1. ". . . quod veritas
prima est objectum fidei, secundum quod ipsa
est non visa, et ea quibus propter ipsam
inhaeretur; et secundum hoc oportet quod
ipsa veritas prima se habeat ad actum fidei
per modum finis secundum rationem rei non
visae; quod pertinet ad rationem rei speratae;"

59. *Sum. Theol.*, II-II, q 2, a 9. "Ipsum autem
credere, est actus intellectus assentientis

veritati divinae ex imperio voluntatis a Deo
motae per gratiam; et sic subjacet libero
arbitrio in ordine ad Deum."

Sum. Theol., II-II, q 4, a 3. "Manifestum est
. . . quod actus fidei ordinatur ad objectum
voluntatis, quod est bonum, sicut ad finem.
Hoc autem bonum quod est finis fidei, scilicet
bonum divinum, est proprium objectum
charitatis. Et ideo charitas dicitur forma fidei,
inquantum per charitatem actus fidei perfici-
tur et formatur."

60. *Cont. Gent.*, II, 48, 4. "A conceptione uni-
versali non sequitur motus et actio, nisi
mediante particulari apprehensione, eo quod
motus et actio erga particularia est. Intellectus
autem naturaliter est universalium apprehen-
sivus. Ad hoc igitur quod ex apprehensione
intellectus sequatur motus aut quaecumque
actio, oportet quod universalis intellectus
conceptio applicetur ad particularia."

61. *Sum. Theol.*, I-II, q 18, a 1.

62. Intellect in seizing the good seizes the
presence of being to appetite. Cf. C. O'Neil,
"St. Thomas and the Nature of Man," in *Proceedings of the American Catholic Philosophical Association*, 1951, pp. 58-59. He stresses
that being is present in its own way to

appetite. As St. Thomas says the actual being
of a thing is what is perfective of appetite.
The problem is to say how the actual existence (ontological existence) or being as good
is incorporated into moral good which is also
immediately given. Cf. also the discussion on
the end of man in A. C. Pegis and G. Smith
in the *Proceedings of the American Catholic
Philosophical Association,* Boston, 1949.

63. *Sum. Theol.,* I-II, q 5, a 5, ad 1. "Dicendum,
quod sicut natura non deficit homini in necessariis, quamvis non dederit ipsi arma et
tegumenta, sicut aliis animalibus, quia dedit
ei rationem et manus quibus possit haec sibi
acquirere: ita nec deficit homini in necessariis,
quamvis non daret ipsi aliquod principium
quo posset beatitudinem consequi; hoc enim
erat impossibile; sed dedit ei liberum arbitri-
um, quo possit converti ad Deum qui eum
faceret beatum. "Quae enim per amicos
possumus, per nos aliqualiter possumus," ut
dicitur in III Ethica, cap. III, post med."

64. For a discussion of the norms of morality
and the norm of morality in St. Thomas, Cf.
O. Lottin, *Principes de Morale,* Tome I et II,
especially Tome II, pp. 115-125 and 127-137.
He stresses that St. Thomas speaks about end

and right reason (recta ratio). End refers to the ultimate end. Right reason is natural reason or the first principles of natural reason. What we have tried to show is that reason as reason implies an object, and as right reason implies the impulsion of the good. It has to do with reason as practical. Reason cannot be just the form of man; it is this form as knowing, as having being and the good. The rational man must appreciate existence: what is; he must always love that. But he must, in the situation he is in, view modes of being, as they are suitable to or useful for maintaining himself as a rational being, but also as they are in themselves for only thus can they ultimately be seen as incorporated in that which Is and Is Good in Itself. Lottin says clearly enough that the first practical principle is an expression of being. But one has a feeling that reason is seen too much as nature and the nature is the norm. But the nature of reason is first of all that sort of nature that is a knowing and loving nature so that being and end are included in it as nature.

Cf. V. Bourke, *St. Thomas and the Greek Moralists*, pp. 21-29. Dr. Bourke stresses here, as few do, that the rule of morality is connected with speculative philosophy. He makes

clearer, I think, than Père Lottin that right
reason has an object and this object is very
important when speaking of reason as the
norm. When man doesn't see clearly his last
end he yet can act reasonably, or be turned
the right way. He can distinguish in varying
degrees of clearness the object of reason. The
metaphysician should try to see what this
object should be, in even considering the right
means to the last end.

I have tried to show what is the object of
speculative reason in its highest knowledge
and how the concrete good, as the incentive
to action, the concern of practical reason
comes under the regulation of the speculative
object. Also I am speaking here of only a
temporary end—not strictly of means.
Cf. L. Kendzierski, *Proceedings of the
American Catholic Philosophical Association*
(XXIV), 1950, pp. 102-110. Here we are
considering only moral goodness as expressed
in the first principle. Dr. Kendzierski speaks
of it on p. 106.

The first practical principle is under the
impulsion of the good. It expresses it: do
good. But what is this good? Goodness of
the will depends upon the object and the
object comes from the reason as we have

shown. But then to say that reason is the form of man and the good is what suits it according to the form, might leave this good indefinite. Reason can be seen simply as form, but it should also be seen as in act knowing its object, its end, and this could be the true as such or more correctly it should be the good as true or being in its actuality as that which can be the object of the will. Thus it is under the impulsion of being as being in its actuality and totality which is good—that intellect turns to the work to be done. It is the good that makes what is to be done an end to be done and under it it becomes end and good. Being, as actual at some level is what all things seek, but reason seeks only what is good as good. Thus the first principle is the **affirmation of being as good or the existent as good.** And all other things must be brought under it as some participation in existence actually understood. If all things are to be according to reason they are all to be seen as participating in, or ordered to, some totality of being—not just to the form of man as form.

65. *Sum. Theol.*, q 2, a 7. "Via autem hominibus veniendi ad beatitudinem est mysterium incarnationis et passionis Christi."

The Aquinas Lectures

Published by the Marquette University Press,
Milwaukee 3, Wisconsin

St. Thomas and the Life of Learning (1937) by
the late Fr. John F. McCormick, S.J., professor of philosophy at Loyola University.

St. Thomas and the Gentiles (1938) by Morti-
mer J. Adler, Ph.D., associate professor of
the philosophy of law, University of Chicago.

St. Thomas and the Greeks (1939) by Anton C.
Pegis, Ph.D., president of the Pontifical Institute of Mediaeval Studies, Toronto.

The Nature and Functions of Authority (1940)
by Yves Simon, Ph.D., professor of philosophy of social thought, University of Chicago.

St. Thomas and Analogy (1941) by Fr. Gerald
B. Phelan, Ph.D., director of the Mediaeval
Institute, University of Notre Dame.

St. Thomas and the Problem of Evil (1942) by
Jacques Maritain, Ph.D., professor of philosophy, Princeton University.

Humanism and Theology (1943) by W e r n e r
Jaeger, Ph.D., Litt.D., "university" professor,
Harvard University.

The Nature and Origins of Scientism (1944) by Fr. John Wellmuth, S.J., Chairman of the Department of Philosophy, Xavier University.

Cicero in the Courtroom of St. Thomas Aquinas (1945) by the late E. K. Rand, Ph.D., Litt.D., LL.D., Pope Professor of Latin, *emeritus,* Harvard University.

St. Thomas and Epistemology (1946) by Fr. Louis-Marie Régis, O.P., Th.L., Ph.D., director of the Albert the Great Institute of Mediaeval Studies, University of Montreal.

St. Thomas and the Greek Moralists (1947, Spring) by Vernon J. Bourke, Ph.D., professor of philosophy, St. Louis University, St. Louis, Missouri.

History of Philosophy and Philosophical Education (1947, Fall) Étienne Gilson of the Académie française, director of studies and professor of the history of mediaeval philosophy, Pontifical Institute of Mediaeval Studies, Toronto.

The Natural Desire for God (1948) by Fr. William R. O'Connor, S.T.L., Ph.D., professor of dogmatic theology, St. Joseph's Seminary, Dunwoodie, N. Y.

St. Thomas and The World State (1949) by Robert M. Hutchins, Chancellor of The University of Chicago.

Methods in Metaphysics (1950) by Fr. Robert J. Henle, S.J., Dean of tthe Graduate School, St. Louis University, St. Louis, Missouri.

Wisdom and Love in St. Thomas Aquinas (1951) by Étienne Gilson of the Académie française, director of studies and professor of the history of mediaeval philosophy, Pontifical Institute of Mediaeval Studies, Toronto.

The Good in Existential Metaphysics (1952) by Elizabeth G. Salmon, associate professor of philosophy in the Graduate School of Fordham University.

First in Series (1937) $1.00; all others $2.00
Uniform format, cover and binding.